PUBLISHED BY
Bob Adams, Inc.
260 Center Street
Holbrook, MA 02343
All rights reserved. No part of this
book may be reproduced in any
form or by any means without
permission in writing from the
author.

ACKNOWLEDGEMENTS
Many thanks to Andrew Mowbray,
Nicholas Nerich, Ann DeAngelis,
Kathleen MacDonald, Robert
Oakes, Ronald Bizier and Thomas
Franke, who all helped put this
book together.

A special thanks to my daughter,
Polly, who wouldn't let me quit.

Segregansett Country Club "Seggy"
is the track that inspired this
ballad. Seggy is located in Dighton,
Massachusetts and was
incorporated on December 2, 1899.
It was one of the early country
clubs founded during the golden
era of golf in the United States and
was a charter member of the
Massachusetts Golf Association.

Prologue

This tale portrays an unsung guy;
It speaks to you and me
Of ninety-nine and pressure shots
And anguish on the tee.

To beat the course? To win the match?
That's not the game we play.
It's us we face out on the tee,
The guy to beat each day.

To hear the crack,
   to know the feel,
When you've just
   timed the swing,
Golf brings a glow
   of happiness
No other
   sport can bring.

But Scotland's game is tough to learn
That glow is hard to find.
How many try and walk away
Too taxing for the mind.

The words you hear
    along the way,
So many moods
    to tame,
To keep it in
    when it wants out
And no one
    else to blame.

The players talk
   of legs that move,
And shoulder turn
   and feet.
The hips move first,
   Before the arms,
And clubface speed
   to meet.

My day arrived – at last the groove,
The shots were sharp and crisp.
A forty-footer fell on four,
Chipped in on number six.

I can recall each shot I made;
The hole, the spot, the lie,
The fairway woods, that bunker shot,
The putts that didn't die.

And even when
   I bombed on Eight,
They knew
   I was no snap.
"Nine shots," they laughed,
   "We know your aim,
Protect that
   handicap."

My ball alone the front side won.
They marveled at my play.
"Your best before was one-o-four?"
The losers said, "No way!"

We paused at Ten, to feel the day.
Life is a great design
The grass, the sky, the foliage;
The card read forty-nine.

But no one sports the "Masters Coat"
  Reflecting on the past,
For winners win who concentrate
  Each shot until the last.

At Twelve I knew the die was cast.
The course must be attacked,
For ninety-nine was in my sight
There was no turning back.

The Thirteenth fell with no finesse,
A routine bogie four.
I knew at last what winners feel,
Euphoric with the score.

But Fourteen plays
    with fear up front,
It costs you left and right.
They tell of some,
    who broke right here,
Still cry out in the night.

With poise I parred, could it be true
With four holes left to taste?
Two fours, a three and then the five,
With six big shots to waste.

At tight Fifteen I gave two back,
But still had four in hand.
Why let the thought of doubt sneak out
And turn the Grail to sand?

The Sixteenth tee
was where it struck
The inner
voice of fear,
"You don't get back
what's gone away,"
I heard it
loud and clear.

It went so quick, that picture swing,
The thought raced through my mind,
"No, not again, you've come so far,
Don't think of ninety-nine."

At Seventeen hands turn to ice
And throats close shut with fright,
For water, wood and sand surround
This masochist's delight.

The supple turn was jerky now.
The nerves had come unstuck.
With muffled sob I hit the fourth
Up on the green by luck.

Somehow it fell, a backdoor putt,
With five I left the green.
They shook their heads in disbelief
As we headed for Eighteen.

The par five hole with none to spare,
The test was up to me.
The ghosts of all who came before
Were waiting on the tee.

You've all been there – the needed par,
The practice swing so grand,
The pause to check; to fix the flight,
The waggle, check the hands.

The dimples glared
against the green,
The birds
too scared to fly.
Like tempered steel
I curled it back,
Then thunder
pierced the sky.

The mind's
   the game
It's all upstairs.
   I knew the shot by sound ...
A dying quail
   hit from the top,
They found it out of
   bounds.

No one can help, the job is done,
You must accept the blow.
You've failed, you're bad,
You've missed the mark,
There'll be no "How to go!"

What brings
us back?
What soothes
the heart?
What calms
the livid hack?
What makes
us pay
the weekly
price
To smile at
every crack?

We just dismiss
   the final score,
To stop the
   awful pain.
All double bogies
   turn to pars,
The good shots
   entertained.

The "ifs" and "buts"
   are cancelled out
So it won't
   sound so bad.
You hear the tale
   at every club,
"Without the, I'da had…"

Though ninety-nine
    waits at the course
It's still within my play
We're down again
    for nine A.M.,
Tomorrow
    is the day!

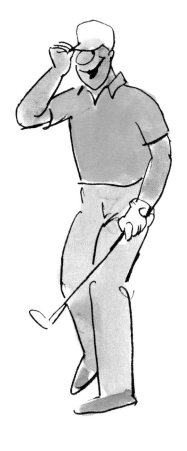